TURMERIC COOKBOOK

55 TURMERIC RECIPES FOR ENERGY, HEALTH & LONGEVITY

K. HELMSTETTER

Green Butterfly Press

ABOUT THE AUTHOR

Kristen Helmstetter is an author traveling the world with her family on a multi-year odyssey to experience other cultures and stay fit while she stuffs her face with their food. (For now, meat anyway.)

See Kristen's blog at:

GlobalKristen.com

Twitter: @KristensRaw

Instagram: global_kristen

Copyright © 2018 Kristen Suzanne Helmstetter

All rights reserved. No part of this book shall be reproduced, stored in a retrieval system, or transmitted by any means, electronic, mechanical, photocopying, recording, or otherwise, without written permission from the publisher. Although every precaution has been taken in the preparation of this book, the publisher and author assume no responsibility for errors or omissions. Nor is any liability assumed for damages resulting from the use of the information contained herein.

For information on excerpting, reprinting or licensing portions of this book, please write to kristen@globalkristen.com.

CONTENTS

Also by K. Helmstetter — ix
Introduction — xi

PART I
BEVERAGES

Tasty Turmeric Almond Milk	2
Electric Turmeric Lemonade	4
Warming Cinnamon Golden Milk	5
1-Minute Turmeric Pecan Milk	6
Pumpkin Spice Buttered Latte	7
Tropical Turmeric Frosty	8
Brain Power Turmeric Cubes (for Coffee or Tea)	9
Delicate Turmeric 'n' Cream Tea	11
Powered-Up Immune Juice Shot	12
Anti-Inflammatory Turmeric Iced Milk	13
Cooling Turmeric Lassi	14
Turmeric Buttered Matcha Latte	15
Turmeric Hot Cocoa	17
Turmeric Protein Iced Coffee	19
Spicy Egg Turmeric Coffee	20
Blueberry 'n' Cranberry Turmeric Yogurt Smoothie	21

PART II
BREAKFAST

Turmeric Cayenne Spiced French Toast	25
Turmeric Paleo Blender Pancakes (Gluten-free)	27
Turmeric Chocolate Chip Granola	29
Oatmeal au Turmeric	31
Turmeric Scrambled Eggs	32

PART III
SIDES & SNACKS

Veggie Turmeric Cream Cheese Spread	34
Rosemary Turmeric Compound Butter	36
Turmeric Cottage Cheese	38
Turmeric Dusted Toast	40
Turmeric Cinnamon Vanilla Shoestring Yams	41
Sunset Turmeric Rice	43
Creamy Turmeric Mac 'n' Cheese	44
Turmeric Mustard Sardine Pate	46
No-Mayo Deviled Eggs with Turmeric	47
Turmeric Buttered Mashed Potatoes	49
Roasted Brussels Sprouts with Turmeric	50
Turmeric Buttered Broccoli = "Rice"	51
Roasted Kale Chips with Coconut, Turmeric, and Ghee	52
Turmeric and Fennel Seed Caramelized Onions	54
Turmeric Buttered Pumpkin Puree	55

PART IV
ENTREES

Gently Baked Chili Powder Turmeric Wild-Caught Salmon	58
Easy Slow Cooker Turmeric "Kalua" Shredded Pork	60
One-Pot Turmeric Brats	62
Garlic Turmeric Meatballs	64
Turmeric Marinara	66

PART V
SALADS & DRESSING

Turmeric Citrus Dressing	70
Creamy Turmeric Olive Oil Dressing	72
Tahini Turmeric Spicy Dressing	73

PART VI
SOUPS

Turmeric-Root Healing Soup	76
Roasted Cauliflower and Carrot Soup	78
Broccoli Turmeric Ginger Soup	80

PART VII
DESSERTS

Chocolate Chip Golden Ice Cream	84
Pumpkin Spice Turmeric Chia Pudding	86
Cherry Chocolate Turmeric Chia Pudding	87
Almond Coconut Turmeric Date Bars (No-Bake)	89
Turmeric Honey-Sweetened Whipped Cream	91
Turmeric Molasses Pumpkin Pie	92
Turmeric Chocolate Chip Fruit Mash	94

PART VIII
HEALTH

Turmeric Whitening Tooth Paste	96
Turmeric Olive Oil Pulling	98
Turmeric Ginger Tincture	100

Conclusion & Free PDF   103

ALSO BY K. HELMSTETTER

Matcha Cookbook: 55 Matcha Recipes for Energy, Health & Longevity

INTRODUCTION

I'd like to send you a free gift, my ebook, *Easy Gluten-Free Cookbook*. Just email me at kristen@globalkristen.com and mention the title of this book (Turmeric Cookbook).

∼

I've been having a love affair with turmeric for the past year. Turmeric, a popular spice in Indian curry recipes, is one of my favorites because of its vibrant yellow/orange hue, earthy flavor, and medicinal properties.

Turmeric is quickly growing in popularity as scientists research its many health boosting properties, specifically the component of turmeric known as curcumin. This is a powerful antioxidant reputed to lower the levels of inflammation, making it anti-inflammatory, especially for chronic inflammation which can lead to various diseases like cancer, cardiovascular disease, neurological disease, type-2 diabetes, and arthritis.

With the increasing number of studies showcasing health benefits of curcumin, it's no surprise that people want more ways to get this health booster into their diet. I, too, use turmeric as culinary medicine to boost my longevity and health, especially my brain health. I even travel with it in my purse so I can add it to meals at restaurants.

The recipes in this book provide a variety of ways to help you get turmeric, and therefore, curcumin, into your diet on a more regular basis.

Though I mostly just use it as a powdered spice added to food, you can make a medicinal tincture, consume the fresh root, or even add the essential oil to recipes. They're all beneficial and good.

This book will introduce you to making a medicinal tincture, using the fresh and vibrant root, and giving the option of exploring turmeric's anti-microbial and potent anti-inflammatory properties via turmeric essential oil (available from LivingLibations.com), but, primarily, we're using ground turmeric (or curcumin extract) powder as a spice in cooking.

When I use the powder as a spice, I like using "curcumin extract" powder to get the most medicinal benefits of turmeric because it's concentrated (available from LongevityWarehouse.com). Sometimes you'll see a range for the amount of turmeric; powder in the recipes. If you're new to it you might try the low end of the range and build up as you see fit.

Also, you'll see black pepper listed in most of the recipes, even sweet ones. This isn't always used for flavoring; in fact, we add black pepper when using turmeric to increase the bioavailability of the turmeric.

PART I
BEVERAGES

TASTY TURMERIC ALMOND MILK

Yield 1 quart

I make my own fresh homemade almond milk, because it doesn't have risky preservatives or emulsifiers. You can use this milk in protein shakes, soups, oatmeal, ice creams, or just drink a glass of it over ice.

- *1 cup raw organic almonds*
- *water (for soaking)*

- *4 cups water (for blending)*
- *1 tablespoon ground turmeric (or curcumin extract) powder*
- *2 pinches freshly ground black pepper*
- *1 pinch sea salt*

Place the almonds in a bowl and fill with water to cover the almonds, by about a half inch. Let them soak overnight. The following morning, drain off and discard the water. Rinse the almonds.

Place the almonds and a fresh quart of water in a blender. Add the turmeric, black pepper, and salt. Blend on high for about a minute.

Using a nut milk bag, strain the milk into a pitcher or bowl, and discard the pulp left in the nut milk bag. Store the almond milk in the refrigerator for up to five days. Natural almond milk will separate so give it shake before using.

Variation: Add 1/2 teaspoon vanilla bean powder.

ELECTRIC TURMERIC LEMONADE

Yield 3 cups

I use the word "electric" because the color is so vibrant it lights up the room.

- 2 1/2 cups water
- 1/2 cup fresh lemon juice
- zest from half of a lemon
- 2 tablespoons raw honey, more to taste
- 1/2 teaspoon turmeric (or curcumin extract) powder

Blend everything. Serve chilled.

WARMING CINNAMON GOLDEN MILK

Yield 1 serving

Wind down your evening with this wonderful milk.

- *1 cup milk of choice*
- *1 teaspoon grass-fed organic ghee*
- *1/2 teaspoon ground turmeric (or curcumin extract) powder*
- *1/2 teaspoon ground cinnamon powder*
- *1 pinch freshly ground black pepper*
- *3 to 5 drops vanilla liquid stevia extract (or other choice of sweetener)*

In a small sauce pan, warm the milk to about 130 degrees F. Transfer the warmed milk to a blender and add the remaining ingredients. Blend briefly.

1-MINUTE TURMERIC PECAN MILK

Yield 1 serving

Drink this straight up or use in smoothies, soups, and other recipes calling for a milk.

- *1 cup water*
- *1 to 2 tablespoons (unsalted) pecan nut butter*
- *1/4 to 1/2 teaspoon ground turmeric (or curcumin extract) powder*
- *1 pinch freshly ground black pepper*
- *1 pinch sea salt*

Blend everything until smooth.

PUMPKIN SPICE BUTTERED LATTE

Yield 1 to 2 servings

This recipe will remind you of autumn and the fall holidays.

- 2 cups freshly brewed hot coffee
- 2 tablespoons grass-fed (unsalted) butter
- 1/2 cup canned (or freshly cooked) pumpkin puree
- 1/2 teaspoon ground pumpkin spice powder
- 1/4 to 1/2 teaspoon ground turmeric (or curcumin extract) powder
- 2 raw pasture-raised, organic egg yolks
- 1 pinch freshly ground black pepper
- 3 to 5 drops liquid vanilla stevia

Blend everything together until creamy.

TROPICAL TURMERIC FROSTY

Yield 1 serving

You'll love this recipe on a hot summer day.

- *1 cup milk of choice*
- *1 cup frozen pineapple*
- *3/4 cup frozen mango*
- *2 tablespoons dried, shredded, and unsweetened coconut*
- *1/2 to 1 teaspoon ground turmeric (or curcumin extract) powder*
- *1 pinch freshly ground black pepper*

Blend everything together.

BRAIN POWER TURMERIC CUBES (FOR COFFEE OR TEA)

Yield 16 Brain Power Turmeric Cubes (depending on your silicone mold)

Inspired by Dave Asprey's Bulletproof Coffee™ where he blends grass-fed butter and his Brain Octane™ MCT oil (an extra potent form of MCT oil) into coffee, I followed suit but added a few more health enhancers. Then, to make the process super quick and convenient for people on the go, I mixed up a large batch and froze them into square molds. Now, I can quickly blend one into my hot coffee each morning in seconds.

- *16 tablespoons grass-fed (unsalted) butter*
- *10 tablespoons Brain Octane* (or MCT oil)*
- *6 tablespoons raw cacao butter*
- *1 tablespoon vanilla bean powder*
- *1 tablespoon ground turmeric (or curcumin extract) powder*
- *1 to 2 teaspoons freshly ground black pepper*

Warm the ingredients in a small pot, over low heat, stirring as needed, until liquid. Pour the mixture into a silicone mold(s), stirring the mixture in the pot, as needed, to ensure the spices don't fall to the bottom of the pot. Freeze them overnight. Pop the cubes out of the silicone mold and onto a plate so the turmeric doesn't stain your counter. Transfer to a glass container (or re-sealable freezer bag), and store in the freezer.

To use in coffee, place a cube in your blender. Add up to 16 ounces of freshly brewed hot coffee. Blend.

* You can buy Brain Octane at UpgradedSelf.com.

DELICATE TURMERIC 'N' CREAM TEA

Yield 1 serving

When you're in the mood for something soft, light, and warm, make this tea.

- *1 cup hot water*
- *1/4 teaspoon ground turmeric (or curcumin extract) powder*
- *1 pinch freshly ground black pepper*
- *1 splash of grass-fed heavy cream*
- *sweetener, if desired*

Blend everything together.

POWERED-UP IMMUNE JUICE SHOT

Yield 1 to 2 cups

If I'm feeling any cold or flu symptoms coming on, or if I'm around anyone who is sick, I load up on this potent juice shot.

- *8 ounces fresh turmeric root*
- *4 to 8 ounces fresh ginger root*
- *1 large lemon, quartered*

Juice the ingredients in a juicer. Drink a couple ounces a few times a day, if you're under the weather.

Variation: Add raw honey and coconut oil for additional anti-viral boosts.

ANTI-INFLAMMATORY TURMERIC ICED MILK

Yield 1 serving

This recipe has a kick and is good for toning down inflammation.

- 1 cup grass-fed, whole-fat milk (or coconut milk)
- 1-inch fresh ginger root, peeled and chopped
- 1/2 teaspoon ground turmeric (or curcumin extract) powder
- 1/4 teaspoon ground cardamom powder
- 1 pinch freshly ground black pepper
- 1/8 teaspoon ground cayenne pepper powder (more to taste)
- 1/8 teaspoon vanilla bean powder
- 1 to 3 teaspoons raw honey
- 1 cup ice

Blend everything until smooth.

COOLING TURMERIC LASSI

Yield 1 to 2 servings

I like this recipe for breakfast.

- *1 cup grass-fed, whole-fat yogurt (or unsweetened kefir)*
- *1 teaspoon ground turmeric (or curcumin extract) powder*
- *1/4 cup pomegranate juice (unsweetened)*
- *zest of 1/2 orange*
- *1 whole orange, peeled*
- *1/4 cup water, more if needed*
- *1 pinch freshly ground black pepper*
- *1 drop turmeric essential oil (optional)*

Blend everything together.

TURMERIC BUTTERED MATCHA LATTE

Yield 1 serving

Matcha tea, a nutritious Japanese tea ceremony beverage, is basically green tea on steroids. The difference between matcha and regular green tea is that, with matcha tea, the leaves are ground into a powder and consumed "whole" instead of steeped. This makes a powerful drink for both mind and body. Matcha green tea powder has antioxidants, chlorophyll, vitamins, and can benefit your body in a number of ways. I like it so much that I wrote a whole ebook filled with recipes: *Matcha Cookbook*.

- *1 1/2 cups water*
- *1/2 teaspoon matcha green tea powder*
- *1 tablespoon grass-fed (unsalted) butter*
- *1/2 teaspoon ground turmeric (or curcumin extract) powder*
- *1 pinch freshly ground black pepper*
- *1/4 teaspoon vanilla bean powder*
- *sweetener, optional*

Heat the water on a stove until it reaches 175 degrees F. Transfer to a blender and add the remaining ingredients. Blend.

TURMERIC HOT COCOA

Yield 1 serving

Sometimes you just want a nice cup of cocoa. Adding turmeric makes it extra healthy.

- *1 cup grass-fed, whole-fat milk (or milk of choice)*
- *1/2 teaspoon ground turmeric (or curcumin extract) powder*

- *2 teaspoons cocoa powder*
- *2 teaspoons maple syrup*
- *1 pinch freshly ground black pepper*

Blend everything to mix. Transfer the milk mixture to a small pot on the stove and warm to desired temperature.

TURMERIC PROTEIN ICED COFFEE

Yield 1 serving

This recipe was inspired by Dave Asprey's delicious Bulletproof Coffee™ of BulletproofExec.com.

- 1 1/2 to 2 cups freshly brewed coffee
- 2 tablespoons grass-fed collagen protein powder
- 1 to 2 tablespoons grass-fed (unsalted) butter
- 1 tablespoon MCT oil (or coconut oil)
- 1/4 to 1 teaspoon ground turmeric (or curcumin extract) powder
- 1 pinch freshly ground black pepper
- 1 cup ice

Blend everything together except for the ice. Place the ice in a large glass (we use a quart-size glass mason jar) and pour the coffee mixture on top.

SPICY EGG TURMERIC COFFEE

Yield 1 serving

Raw egg yolks that are pasture-raised and organic are healthy. Adding them to coffee is one of my favorite ways to get them in my diet. I also love MCT and coconut oils... coconut is anti-inflammatory and so good for the brain.

- *2 cups freshly brewed hot coffee*
- *2 tablespoons grass-fed (unsalted) butter*
- *1 tablespoon MCT oil (or coconut oil)*
- *1/4 teaspoon vanilla bean powder*
- *1/8 to 1/4 teaspoon ground cayenne pepper powder*
- *1/4 to 1/2 teaspoon ground turmeric (or curcumin extract) powder*
- *1 pinch freshly ground black pepper*
- *2 raw pasture-raised, organic egg yolks*

Blend everything, except for the egg yolks, until smooth. Add the yolks and blend briefly to mix.

BLUEBERRY 'N' CRANBERRY TURMERIC YOGURT SMOOTHIE

Yield 1 serving

This is a healthy smoothie that's perfect for a quick breakfast or mid-day snack.

- *1 cup whole-fat, grass-fed, plain yogurt*
- *1/3 cup frozen blueberries*
- *1/2 cup frozen cranberries*
- *1/2 teaspoon ground turmeric (or curcumin extract) powder*
- *5 drops liquid vanilla stevia, more to taste*

Blend everything together.

PART II
BREAKFAST

TURMERIC CAYENNE SPICED FRENCH TOAST

Yield 2 servings

This French toast is special... the hint of cayenne spice makes it a bit more grown up.

- *4 slices of sourdough bread (or gluten-free bread)*
- *grass-fed ghee, for cooking*
- *2 pasture-raised, organic eggs*

- *1/2 cup grass-fed whipping cream*
- *1/2 teaspoon ground cinnamon powder*
- *1/2 teaspoon ground turmeric (or curcumin extract) powder*
- *1/8 teaspoon cayenne pepper, more to taste**
- *1 pinch sea salt*
- *1 pinch freshly ground black pepper*
- *grass-fed butter and maple syrup, for toppings*

Whisk everything together, except for the ghee, in a shallow dish. Dip each slice of bread into the mixture and then place them in baking dish. Pour rest of the egg mixture on top, and let them soak for a couple of minutes.

Heat a skillet over medium heat with a teaspoon (or two) of ghee. Remove the soaking bread and transfer it to the skillet, and cook 2 to 3 minutes per side, in batches if needed. Serve with butter and maple syrup.

* If making for kids you might consider omitting the cayenne.

TURMERIC PALEO BLENDER PANCAKES (GLUTEN-FREE)

Yield 3 to 5 pancakes

These are good. I mean, who doesn't like pancakes???

- *1 banana, peeled*
- *2 pasture-raised, organic eggs*
- *1/4 teaspoon vanilla bean powder*
- *1/2 teaspoon ground cinnamon powder*
- *1/4 teaspoon ground turmeric (or curcumin extract) powder*
- *1 tablespoon flax seeds*
- *1 tablespoon coconut flour*
- *1 pinch sea salt*
- *grass-fed ghee, for cooking*
- *grass-fed butter and maple syrup for toppings*

Blend the ingredients together. Heat a teaspoon of ghee in a skillet, over medium heat (I like using a cast iron skillet for pancakes). Pour about a 1/4-cup of pancake batter into the skillet. Let the pancake cook for a minute or two, depending on the level of heat used.

When it's ready, flip the pancake (look for little bubbles forming on top of the pancakes). Cook the other side for a minute or so. Stack 'em up on a plate and serve with butter and grade B maple syrup (or raw honey).

TURMERIC CHOCOLATE CHIP GRANOLA

Yield 6 cups

This granola will make your house smell like candy. The secret to this granola? Using Ancient Organic's grass-fed ghee and maple syrup. Shhhhh... don't tell.

- 3 cups old-fashioned oats
- 1 1/2 cups large coconut flakes, dried and unsweetened
- 2 cups chopped pecans
- 2 cups raw sunflower seeds
- 2/3 cup (Ancient Organics*) grass-fed ghee, melted
- 1 tablespoon ground turmeric (or curcumin extract) powder
- 2/3 cup grade B maple syrup, more to taste
- 1 teaspoon sea salt
- 10 to 12 grinds of freshly ground black pepper
- 1 teaspoon ground cinnamon powder
- 1 1/2 teaspoons vanilla bean powder
- 1 cup organic raisins
- 1 cup dark (fair trade) chocolate chips

Preheat the oven to 250 degrees F.

Line two baking sheets with parchment paper. If possible use baking sheets that have a lip around the edge to prevent the granola from falling off as you stir it while it's baking.

Stir the gluten-free oats, coconut flakes, pecans, and sunflower seeds together in a large bowl and set aside. Gently warm the organic grass-fed ghee on the stove and stir in the turmeric, maple syrup, sea salt, black pepper, cinnamon, and vanilla powder. Pour the ghee mixture on top of the oat mixture and stir well to combine everything.

Divide the granola between the two baking sheets. Cook for 1 hour and 15 minutes, stirring every 15 minutes. Remove the granola from the oven and transfer to a large bowl to cool. Add the raisins and chocolate chips. Mix to distribute evenly.

* Ancient Organics ghee is the only ghee I'll use. It has the most superior flavor. You can buy it on Amazon.com or AncientOrganics.com

OATMEAL AU TURMERIC

Yield 1 serving

Even though my family doesn't eat grains often, I sure appreciate a bowl of oatmeal once in a while. It's comfort food.

- *1 serving oatmeal, freshly cooked*
- *1 tablespoon grass-fed butter*
- *1/4 teaspoon ground turmeric (or curcumin extract) powder*
- *1 to 2 tablespoons raisins*
- *1/8 teaspoon ground allspice powder*

Cook the oatmeal per the manufacturer's instructions. Then, stir in the butter, turmeric, raisins, and allspice.

TURMERIC SCRAMBLED EGGS

Yield 1 serving

One of my favorite meals is a big bowl of scrambled eggs. I can eat them for breakfast, lunch, or dinner.

- *1 tablespoon grass-fed butter (or 1 teaspoon grass-fed ghee)*
- *1/4 teaspoon ground turmeric (or curcumin extract) powder*
- *1 pinch freshly ground black pepper*
- *1 pinch sea salt*
- *3 pasture-raised, organic eggs*

Heat a skillet over medium-low heat and melt the butter. Whisk the remaining ingredients together well. Add the egg mixture to the skillet, and gently cook until lightly scrambled.

PART III
SIDES & SNACKS

VEGGIE TURMERIC CREAM CHEESE SPREAD

Yield 1 1/2 cups

Make this crowd-pleasing, healthy cheese spread for your next party.

- *1 cup (8 ounces) grass-fed cream cheese*
- *1 teaspoon ground turmeric (or curcumin extract) powder*
- *1 teaspoon mustard*

- *3/4 teaspoon capers*
- *1/2 teaspoon fresh lemon zest*
- *2 tablespoons yellow onion, chopped*
- *1/4 cup celery, chopped*
- *1/4 cup chopped orange (or red) bell pepper*
- *1 clove garlic, pressed*
- *1/4 teaspoon dried tarragon*
- *1 pinch sea salt*
- *freshly ground black pepper, to taste*

Put the ingredients in a food processor, fitted with the "S" blade. Puree it to your desired texture. Serve this spread on crackers, sourdough toast, or cucumber slices.

ROSEMARY TURMERIC COMPOUND BUTTER

Yield 4 ounces

This is a great way to get a bit more turmeric into your diet every time you use butter. This is great for enjoying on toast, crackers, and cooking vegetables or ground beef with it.

- *4 ounces grass-fed (salted) butter, room temperature*

- *1 teaspoon ground turmeric (or curcumin extract) powder*
- *1 1/2 teaspoons freshly minced rosemary*

Stir everything together in a small bowl until it's combined. Transfer the butter mixture to a piece of parchment paper. Using the parchment paper, gently roll the butter into a log shape as best you can. Place in the refrigerator to get firm.

TURMERIC COTTAGE CHEESE

Yield 1 to 2 servings

This recipe was inspired by Dr. Budwig's cancer protocol where they consume flax oil and cottage cheese. I'm adding extra immune boosting ingredients to mine.

- 1/2 cup grass-fed cottage cheese (not non-fat)
- 1 tablespoon organic flax seed oil*
- 1/4 teaspoon ground turmeric (or curcumin extract) powder
- 1 pinch freshly ground black pepper
- 1 tablespoon freshly ground flax seeds
- 1 tablespoon freshly chopped herbs (basil, oregano, and/or mint are great)
- 1/3 cup organic berries of choice (frozen is fine)
- 1 to 2 teaspoons grade B maple syrup, optional

Using a small food processor, fitted with the "S" blade, process the cottage cheese with the flax oil, turmeric, and black pepper for about 30 seconds. Add the remaining ingredients and process to mix.

* PanaSeeda flax oil, by Activation Products, is the best I've found, available on Amazon.com.

TURMERIC DUSTED TOAST

Yield 1 serving

Good, pure levain sourdough toast is one of my favorite foods, even as a dessert. I'll take it over a slice of cake or pie any day. However, if you're gluten-free, then feel free to use a gluten-free bread.

- *1 slice sourdough bread (or gluten-free bread), toasted*
- *1 to 2 tablespoons grass-fed butter, room temperature*
- *1 pinch sea salt, optional*
- *1/4 teaspoon ground turmeric (or curcumin extract) powder, sifted**
- *freshly ground black pepper*

Spread the butter on your toast, fresh from the toaster. Add salt if desired. Gently sift the turmeric over the toast. Grind black pepper on top.

* Turmeric can make a mess on your countertops so be sure to sift the turmeric onto the toast once the toast is on a plate.

TURMERIC CINNAMON VANILLA SHOESTRING YAMS

Yield 3 to 4 servings

This is my family's favorite way to eat yams or sweet potatoes. If you have leftovers, save them as a cold topping for your next salad.

- *1 large yam or sweet potato, washed*
- *1 1/2 tablespoons ghee, melted*
- *1/2 teaspoon ground turmeric (or curcumin extract) powder*
- *1/4 teaspoon vanilla bean powder*
- *1/4 teaspoon ground cinnamon powder*
- *sea salt, to taste*

- *black pepper, to taste*

Preheat oven to 400 degrees F. Spiralize the sweet potato with a veggie spiralizer into long noodle-like strings. Place them in a bowl and toss to mix with the other ingredients. Spread the mixture onto a large, rimmed baking sheet, and bake for 15 to 20 minutes, or until your desired doneness is reached.

SUNSET TURMERIC RICE

Yield 4 servings

I love rice with lots of butter. I love it even more with turmeric.

- *3 to 3 1/2 cups freshly cooked white rice**
- *1/2 teaspoon ground turmeric (or curcumin extract) powder*
- *freshly ground black pepper, to taste*
- *sea salt, to taste*
- *4 tablespoons grass-fed butter*

While the rice is still warm from cooking, stir in the turmeric, pepper, salt, and butter.

* 1 cup of uncooked white rice yields 3 to 3 1/2 cups cooked.

CREAMY TURMERIC MAC 'N' CHEESE

Yield 4 servings

For those times you need something that's full of comfort goodness.

- 1 (12 ounce box) pasta*
- 1 cup shredded cheese of choice
- 1/2 cup cream cheese
- 1/2 cup grass-fed, whole-fat milk, more as needed
- 3 tablespoons grass-fed butter
- 1 teaspoon ground turmeric (or curcumin extract) powder
- sea salt, to taste
- freshly ground black pepper, to taste

Cook the pasta per the manufacturer's instructions. Once it's strained, return it to the pot with the rest of the ingredients. Stir until thoroughly mixed.

Variation: Add cooked grass-fed ground beef and steamed broccoli after you've finished mixing together the mac 'n' cheese.

* We love Jovial gluten-free pasta.

TURMERIC MUSTARD SARDINE PATE

Yield 2 servings

If you're not eating sardines, then you should start. As a natural source of marine omega-3 fatty acids, I classify them as a superfood, and my family eats them regularly. Because sardines are low in the food chain, they contain among the lowest levels of mercury of any fish commonly eaten by people.

- *2 cans sardines, with skin and bones*
- *1/4 cup chopped bread and butter pickles*
- *1 tablespoon mustard*
- *1 teaspoon capers*
- *1/4 to 1/2 teaspoon ground turmeric (or curcumin extract) powder*
- *1 to 2 dashes hot sauce*

Mash everything up in a bowl.

NO-MAYO DEVILED EGGS WITH TURMERIC

Yield 12 deviled eggs

My family devours these the moment they're made.

- *6 pasture-raised organic eggs, hard-boiled**
- *3 tablespoons grass-fed, whole-fat Greek yogurt***

- *1 tablespoon yellow mustard*
- *3/4 teaspoon ground turmeric (or curcumin extract) powder*
- *1 splash apple cider vinegar*
- *sea salt, to taste*
- *freshly ground black pepper*
- *fresh herbs, optional*

Peel the eggs, and split them in half lengthwise. Gently scoop the yolks into a small mixing bowl. Set the egg whites on a plate and set aside.

Mash the yolks with a potato masher or fork. Stir in the rest of the ingredients. Use a small spoon and scoop the filling gently into each egg white. Add any fresh herbs for garnish.

* To make the hard-boiled eggs…

Use a pot that will hold the eggs in a single layer. Put the eggs in the pot and add enough water to cover by about a half-inch. Put the pot on the stove and bring the water to a boil, or just about. I use an instant-read-thermometer and when the water temperature reaches about 200 degrees F, I go to the next step…

Turn the heat off, remove the pot from the heat, cover the pot, and set your timer for 9 minutes. While the eggs are in the covered pot, make an ice bath by getting a bowl and putting 2 cups of water plus 2 cups of ice in it. When the timer buzzes, remove the eggs and transfer them to the ice bath. Set the timer for 15 minutes. When the timer goes off, the eggs are cooled, and it's time to peel them.

** My favorite brand is Straus and it's one of the reasons this recipe tastes so delicious.

TURMERIC BUTTERED MASHED POTATOES

Yield 5 to 6 servings

You are about to take mashed potatoes to a new level.

- *2 pounds russet potatoes*
- *8 tablespoons grass-fed butter, room temperature*
- *1/2 to 1 teaspoon ground turmeric (or curcumin extract) powder*
- *freshly ground black pepper, to taste*
- *sea salt, to taste*

Peel and chop the potatoes into evenly sized, large chunks. Place them in a pot of cold, salted water. Bring to a boil. Cook for 15 to 20 minutes, or until a knife slides easily into a piece of potato. Transfer the potatoes to a bowl and add the remaining ingredients. Mash everything together to desired consistency.

ROASTED BRUSSELS SPROUTS WITH TURMERIC

Yield 4 servings

Finally, I found a way to roast Brussels sprouts that works every time, thanks to America's Test Kitchen.

- *1 pound Brussels sprouts, halved*
- *1 tablespoon ghee, melted*
- *1 teaspoon ground turmeric (or curcumin extract) powder*
- *2 pinches sea salt*
- *freshly ground black pepper, to taste*
- *2 tablespoons water*

Preheat your oven to 400 degrees F. Place the Brussels sprouts in a bowl. Add the melted ghee, turmeric, sea salt, black pepper, and water. Stir everything together and transfer everything to a rimmed baking sheet (or roasting pan). Cover with aluminum foil. Cook 12 minutes. Remove foil and cook another 12 minutes. Season with more salt, if needed.

TURMERIC BUTTERED BROCCOLI = "RICE"

Yield 3 to 4 servings

Finely chopped broccoli in place of rice is a great alternative.

- *4 tablespoons grass-fed (salted) butter*
- *1 teaspoon ground turmeric (or curcumin extract) powder*
- *freshly ground black pepper, to taste*
- *1/2 red onion, diced*
- *1 head broccoli florets, minced into "rice" (or 2 heads depending on size)*
- *sea salt, to taste*

Using a chef's pan (or a skillet), over medium-low heat, melt the butter with the turmeric and black pepper. Add the onion and cook for 10 minutes, stirring occasionally. Add the broccoli "rice" and a pinch of sea salt, and cook another 5 to 10 minutes, stirring frequently (until the broccoli is a vibrant green color, don't overcook). Season to taste.

ROASTED KALE CHIPS WITH COCONUT, TURMERIC, AND GHEE

Yield 2 servings

In spite of kale being bitter, my daughter likes munching on these as an afternoon snack. Their airy-light texture helps offset the bitterness a bit, and of course, raw honey sweetens them nicely. Warning: your kids hands and face will get temporarily stained yellow from the turmeric. Be sure to give them a napkin when eating them.

- 1 bunch kale, destemmed and roughly chopped or torn
- 2 tablespoons dried coconut, shredded and unsweetened
- 2 tablespoons grass-fed ghee, melted
- 1 teaspoon ground turmeric (or curcumin extract) powder
- 1 pinch sea salt
- 1 pinch freshly ground black pepper
- drizzle raw honey

Preheat the oven to 350 degrees F. While the oven is preheating, wash the kale and dry it well.

Place the kale in a bowl with the coconut, ghee, turmeric, salt and pepper. Toss to ensure the kale is nicely coated with the other ingredients. Place the kale on two baking sheets, if possible, so the pieces aren't crowded. Roast for 10 minutes, or until crispy. Drizzle with raw honey. Season to taste with more salt if needed.

TURMERIC AND FENNEL SEED CARAMELIZED ONIONS

Yield 2 cups

I like having caramelized onions in the fridge to use as toppings for burgers, pasta, or veggie dishes.

- *2 teaspoons grass-fed ghee*
- *1 large yellow onion, sliced*
- *1/4 teaspoon fennel seeds*
- *1/2 teaspoon ground turmeric (or curcumin extract) powder*
- *2 pinches sea salt*
- *2 pinches freshly ground black pepper*

In a skillet, over medium-low heat, melt the ghee. Add the remaining ingredients and cook for 15 to 20 minutes, stirring often.

TURMERIC BUTTERED PUMPKIN PUREE

Yield 2 servings

This is perfect for the fall holidays. If you're cooking for a crowd, simply multiply the recipe. If you didn't know, pumpkin is low in fructose and high in potassium, carotenoids, and antioxidants.

- *1 heaping cup pumpkin puree**
- *3 tablespoons grass-fed butter*
- *1 teaspoon ground turmeric (or curcumin extract) powder*
- *1/2 teaspoon pumpkin pie spice powder*
- *2 pinches freshly ground black pepper*
- *sea salt, to taste*

Warm everything together in a small pot, over low heat, stirring.

* I make fresh pumpkin using a slow cooker. Poke holes in the pumpkin, and cook it in a slow cooker on LOW for 6 to 8 hours. Cut it in half, scoop out the seeds (discarding or roasting them), and scoop out the flesh. Alternatively, you can use canned pumpkin.

PART IV
ENTREES

GENTLY BAKED CHILI POWDER TURMERIC WILD-CAUGHT SALMON

Yield 2 servings

This salmon recipe makes a weekly appearance in our home. It's healthy, easy, and the chili powder takes the flavor over the top. If I haven't bought our wild-caught salmon from the local fisherman at the farmer's market, I buy online from Vital Choice.

Gently Baked Chili Powder Turmeric Wild-Caught Salmon

- 2 (5 to 6 ounces each) pieces wild-caught salmon
- 1 teaspoon extra virgin olive oil
- sea salt (see directions)
- freshly ground black pepper (see directions)
- 1/8 to 1/4 teaspoon chili powder of choice*
- 1/8 to 1/4 teaspoon ground turmeric (or curcumin extract) powder
- 1 to 2 squeezes fresh lemon (or lime) juice
- freshly chopped cilantro, for garnish

Preheat oven to 250 degrees F. Line a baking sheet with parchment paper or aluminum foil. Gently rub each piece of fish with olive oil and sprinkle with sea salt and black pepper, followed by sprinkling the chili powder and turmeric on top.

Bake until your desired internal temperature is reached, about 20 to 25 minutes to reach 120 degrees F for wild-caught fish. Cook longer if desired.

Just before serving, squeeze on fresh lime or lemon juice and top with fresh cilantro.

* My favorite is Simply Organic, which I buy on Amazon.com or at my local Whole Foods Market. It's mild and tasty.

EASY SLOW COOKER TURMERIC "KALUA" SHREDDED PORK

Yield 4 to 6

I love this recipe because it's easy to prepare and full of delicious flavor. I like to serve it with a side of sauerkraut and vegetables.

The ranges in the seasoning ingredients correspond to the size of the pork shoulder used. That said, adjust accordingly to your desires.

- *1 (2 to 4 pounds) pork shoulder, preferably bone-in*
- *1 1/2 to 3 teaspoons smoked sea salt (or regular sea salt)**
- *1/2 to 1 teaspoon freshly ground black pepper*
- *1/2 to 1 teaspoon ground turmeric (or curcumin extract) powder*

Season the pork all over with the smoked sea salt, black pepper, and turmeric. Place the pork in a slow cooker. Cover the slow cooker with the lid, and cook for 8 to 12 hours on LOW.

Remove the pork to a large plate where you can remove the bone and shred the meat using two forks. Put the meat back in the slow cooker and stir to mix with the juices and fat.

* I use a smoked sea salt that is coarsely ground.

ONE-POT TURMERIC BRATS

Yield 4 servings

I like meals where I put everything in one pot and just cook. Easy to assemble and easy clean up. This one, in particular, is super good and has carrots. Did you know that carrots have polyacetylenes which have been shown to inhibit cancer growth.

- *2 carrots, chopped*
- *1 red bell pepper, chopped*
- *4 cups chopped purple cabbage (about 1/2 to 3/4 a small head)*
- *1/4 teaspoon garlic powder*
- *sea salt, to taste*
- *freshly ground black pepper, to taste*
- *4 bratwurst sausages*
- *1 onion, peeled and sliced*
- *1 tablespoon grass-fed ghee, melted*
- *1 tablespoon mustard (plus more to garnish)*
- *1 teaspoon dried oregano*
- *1 teaspoon ground turmeric (or curcumin extract) powder*

- *1 teaspoon freshly chopped rosemary*
- *Greek yogurt, to garnish (if desired)*

Preheat the oven to 400 degrees F.

In a Dutch oven, place the carrot, bell pepper and cabbage. Add the garlic powder and top with a sprinkle of salt and pepper.

Top the veggies with the brats. Then, place the onion on top of the brats.

In a small pot, warm the ghee, mustard, oregano, and turmeric together. Pour the sauce on top, and add the rosemary.

Cook for 45 to 60 minutes, or until the brats reach the temperature you desire. Stir once midway through the cooking time. Taste and season with extra salt if needed. Serve with a dollop of greek yogurt and extra mustard.

GARLIC TURMERIC MEATBALLS

Yield 4 servings

My husband loves when I make meatballs, and he always asks that I make extra so he can have a midnight snack.

- *1 pound grass-fed ground beef*
- *1 pasture-raised organic egg*
- *1/4 cup freshly and finely grated parmesan cheese*
- *1/2 teaspoon garlic powder*
- *1 teaspoon ground turmeric (or curcumin extract) powder*
- *1 teaspoon fresh thyme leaves*
- *freshly ground black pepper, to taste*
- *sea salt (see directions)*

Preheat the oven to 325 degrees F. Line a rimmed baking sheet with aluminum foil or parchment paper.

In a medium bowl, briefly mix by hand all of the ingredients, except for the salt. Gently form the meat mixture into balls using an ice cream scooper and place them on the lined baking sheet. Sprinkle each meatball with a little sea salt.

Bake for 15 to 20 minutes, or until they reach your desired internal temperature.

TURMERIC MARINARA

Yield 5 cups

I'm Italian so it's only natural that I have a delicious marinara sauce up my sleeve. OMG this stuff is amazing.

- *3 tablespoons grass-fed (salted) butter*
- *1/2 large yellow onion, diced*
- *2 teaspoons ground turmeric (or curcumin extract) powder*
- *1 teaspoon dried oregano*
- *1/4 teaspoon ground cinnamon powder*
- *1/4 teaspoon fennel seeds*
- *2 pinches freshly ground black pepper, more to taste*
- *1 pinch red pepper flakes (I like Aleppo pepper flakes)*
- *1 drizzle maple syrup*
- *5 cloves garlic, chopped*
- *2 (18 ounce) jars of crushed tomatoes*
- *1 tablespoon freshly minced rosemary*
- *1/2 cup freshly chopped basil*

Warm the butter in a medium-sized soup pot over medium-low heat. Add the onion, turmeric, oregano, cinnamon, and black and red peppers. Add a few pinches of salt. Sweat and cook the onions for about 15 minutes. Add the maple syrup and garlic and cook another few minutes.

Add the tomatoes and rosemary. Bring the sauce to a simmer, tasting for salt and adjusting as needed. Simmer for at least 30 minutes and up to an hour. Stir in the basil and cook a few more minutes.

Serve over pasta or cooked ground beef and vegetables.

PART V
SALADS & DRESSING

TURMERIC CITRUS DRESSING

Yield 1 cup

Citrus fruits are high in health-boosting flavonoids, and this tasty dressing will help you consume more.

- *1/2 cup extra virgin olive oil*
- *1/4 cup fresh orange juice*
- *2 tablespoons fresh lime juice*

Turmeric Citrus Dressing

- *2 tablespoons fresh lemon juice*
- *1 tablespoon tamari, wheat-free (or coconut aminos)*
- *1 small clove garlic*
- *1 small knob fresh ginger, peeled*
- *1 teaspoon turmeric (or curcumin extract) powder*
- *freshly ground black pepper*
- *drizzle maple syrup or raw honey, to taste*

Blend all of the ingredients together.

CREAMY TURMERIC OLIVE OIL DRESSING

Yield 1 cup

I particularly like this dressing on a salad topped with grass-fed steak.

- *1/2 cup extra virgin olive oil*
- *1/4 cup fresh lemon juice*
- *2 tablespoons strawberry jam*
- *2 tablespoons whole-fat Greek yogurt*
- *1/2 to 1 teaspoon sea salt*
- *1 teaspoon ground turmeric (or curcumin extract) powder*
- *freshly ground black pepper, to taste*

Blend everything together until creamy.

TAHINI TURMERIC SPICY DRESSING

Yield approximately 1 cup

This creamy recipe is delicious as a dip or salad dressing.

- *1/2 cup tahini*
- *1/2 cup water*
- *3 tablespoons fresh lemon juice (or lime juice)*
- *1 teaspoon toasted sesame oil*
- *1 teaspoon turmeric (or curcumin extract) powder*
- *1/4 teaspoon cayenne pepper*
- *1/2 teaspoon sea salt*
- *freshly ground black pepper, to taste*
- *1 drop turmeric essential oil, optional*

Blend everything together until smooth.

PART VI
SOUPS

TURMERIC-ROOT HEALING SOUP

Yield 2 servings

This steaming bowl of goodness improves spirits and health.

- *1 teaspoon grass-fed ghee*
- *1 leek, white part only, sliced*
- *1/2 teaspoon ground turmeric (or curcumin extract) powder*
- *1 teaspoon mix of various spices like fennel seeds, cumin seeds, and ground allspice*
- *1/2 ounce (about an inch long) turmeric root, peeled and grated*
- *1 clove garlic, pressed*
- *sea salt, to taste*
- *freshly ground black pepper, to taste*
- *1 stalk celery, thinly sliced**
- *1 carrot, thinly sliced**
- *1 to 2 tablespoons freshly chopped herbs like oregano, thyme, and/or rosemary*
- *3 cups homemade chicken bone broth (stock)*

In a medium-sized soup pot, heat the ghee over medium-low heat. Add everything except for the broth. Cook for about 5 minutes. Add the broth. Bring to a simmer and cook 5 minutes. Season to taste.

* I use a mandoline to get uniformly thin slices.

ROASTED CAULIFLOWER AND CARROT SOUP

Yield about 2 quarts

I channeled the soup-making genes I got from my dad when creating this recipe.

- 1 bunch carrots (green tops removed)
- 1 head cauliflower, cut into florets
- 3 tablespoons grass-fed ghee, melted and divided
- sea salt, to taste
- freshly ground black pepper, to taste
- 1/2 to 1 teaspoon ground turmeric (or curcumin extract) powder
- 1/2 purple onion, chopped
- 2 cloves garlic, chopped
- 4 cups homemade bone broth (stock) or water*
- 1/2 cup grass-fed, organic heavy cream (or half-n-half)

Preheat the oven to 400 degree F. Place the carrots and cauliflower in a bowl and toss them in 2 tablespoons of the grass-fed ghee, plus a couple pinches of sea salt and black pepper, and the turmeric powder. Roast them for 20 to 30 minutes.

While the veggies are roasting, sweat the onion, over medium-low heat, in a soup pot with the remaining ghee. Add a pinch each of salt and pepper. This should take about 10 minutes. Add the garlic and let it cook for about one minute. Add the broth and bring the mixture to a simmer.

Blend the roasted vegetables with the broth mixture. Do this in batches if needed. Transfer the blended soup back to the soup pot. Stir in the heavy cream. Season with sea salt, to taste.

* The soup will have more flavor if bone broth (i.e., stock) is used, but if water is your choice, then consider more seasoning and some herbs to increase flavor.

BROCCOLI TURMERIC GINGER SOUP

Yield 6 cups

I make this soup for lunch or dinner, saving leftovers for the next day's breakfast.

- 1 pound broccoli florets, steamed
- 3 cups chicken bone broth (stock), warmed to 175 to 180 degrees F
- 6 tablespoons grass-fed butter
- 1 small clove garlic
- 1/2 ounce (1 to 2 inches) turmeric root, peeled
- 1/2 ounce (1 to 2 inches) ginger root, peeled
- 1/2 teaspoon ground turmeric (or curcumin extract) powder
- 1/4 teaspoon cumin seeds
- 1 teaspoon fresh thyme leaves
- 2 to 3 pinches freshly ground black pepper
- sea salt, to taste*

Put everything in a blender and carefully (because it's hot) blend until smooth. Consider doing this in two batches of blending, if you're blender carafe doesn't hold it all safely. Then, you can stir it together in a soup pot to ensure everything is combined.

* If you're using a salted broth then you won't need to add as much salt.

PART VII
DESSERTS

CHOCOLATE CHIP GOLDEN ICE CREAM

Yield 1 quart

This ice cream is addictive. 'Nuff said.

- *2 cups grass-fed whipping cream*
- *1 cup whole-fat Greek yogurt*
- *4 raw pasture-raised, organic egg yolks*
- *1/3 cup raw honey, more to taste*
- *2 teaspoons ground turmeric (or curcumin extract) powder*

- *1/4 teaspoon vanilla bean powder*
- *1 pinch sea salt*
- *2 pinches freshly ground black pepper*
- *1 (2 oz.) dark chocolate bar, chopped (or dark chocolate chips)*

Blend everything except for the chocolate. Pour the mixture into an ice cream making machine, per the manufacturer's instructions. Add the chocolate when allowed (for my machine that's mid-way).

PUMPKIN SPICE TURMERIC CHIA PUDDING

Yield 3 to 4

Chia puddings have an interesting and fun texture.

- 1/2 cup chia seeds
- 2 cups Tasty Turmeric Almond Milk (see recipe, "Beverages" section)
- 2 teaspoons ground pumpkin spice powder
- 1 tablespoon raw honey

Place the chia seeds in a quart-sized glass mason jar. Blend the milk, pumpkin spice powder, and honey together. Add the almond milk mixture to the mason jar with the chia seeds.

Secure a lid tightly and shake vigorously for a moment. Wait a few minutes and shake again. Wait a few more minutes and shake again. Repeat a couple more times. Refrigerate for up to four hours.

CHERRY CHOCOLATE TURMERIC CHIA PUDDING

Yield 2 servings

Chia pudding is one of my husband's favorite snacks. It tastes great and is guilt-free.

- 5 tablespoons chia seeds
- 1 cup milk of choice
- 1/2 cup frozen cherries
- 1 teaspoon ground (or curcumin extract) turmeric
- 1 tablespoon cocoa powder
- 1 pinch freshly ground black pepper
- 1 pinch sea salt
- 2 teaspoons raw honey, more to taste

Place the chia seeds in a quart-sized glass mason jar. Blend the remaining ingredients. Add the milk mixture to the mason jar with the chia seeds.

Secure a lid tightly and shake vigorously for a moment. Wait a few minutes and shake again. Wait a few more minutes and shake again. Repeat a couple more times. Refrigerate for up to four hours.

ALMOND COCONUT TURMERIC DATE BARS (NO-BAKE)

Yield 12 to 15 bars, depending on baking dish size

I love recipes that come together with such ease. These date bars are scrumptious(!) and my family gobbles them up the same day I make them.

- *2 cups raw almonds*
- *1 cup dried coconut, unsweetened and shredded*

- *1 tablespoon ground turmeric (or curcumin extract) powder*
- *1 (3-finger) pinch sea salt*
- *1 (3-finger) pinch freshly ground black pepper*
- *16 Medjool dates, pitted*

Using a food processor, fitted with the "S" blade, process the almonds, coconut, turmeric, salt and pepper to a coarse grind. Add the dates and process until you get a dough that sticks together when you press it between your fingers. Transfer the dough into a baking dish and press down firmly.

TURMERIC HONEY-SWEETENED WHIPPED CREAM

Yield 1 1/2 cups

This gorgeous whipped cream takes less than a minute to make and goes wonderfully on Turmeric Molasses Pumpkin Pie (see recipe, below) or on any fruit, dessert, or coffee beverage.

- *1 1/2 cups grass-fed whipping cream*
- *1 teaspoon ground turmeric (or curcumin extract) powder*
- *1 teaspoon raw honey*

Blend everything, on high, until you hear the whipping cream is done and not whipping anymore. This usually takes my (high-speed) blender less than 30 seconds.

Variation: For a blast of flavor, add one drop of organic orange (or lemon) essential oil.

TURMERIC MOLASSES PUMPKIN PIE

Yield one 8 or 9-inch pie

This pie comes together quickly when using a blender and a pre-made pie crust. I prefer cooling it in the refrigerator overnight to firm up perfectly.

- *3 pasture-raised organic eggs*
- *1/2 cup USA non-GMO birchwood xylitol (or regular sugar)*

Turmeric Molasses Pumpkin Pie

- *2 tablespoons molasses*
- *1 tablespoon ground pumpkin pie spice powder*
- *2 teaspoons ground turmeric (or curcumin extract) powder*
- *2 cups homemade pumpkin pulp puree from a sugar pumpkin (or canned pumpkin)*
- *1 cup grass-fed whipping cream*
- *1/2 teaspoon sea salt*
- *1 pinch freshly ground black pepper*
- *1 uncooked pie crust of choice (I prefer gluten-free)*

Preheat oven to 425 degrees F.

Blend everything together and pour the filling into an uncooked pie shell. Bake for 15 minutes. Lower the temperature to 325 degrees F. Bake an additional 45 to 55 minutes (until a knife inserted comes out clean). About halfway through cooking time put on a pie shield.

Turn the oven off, crack the oven door open, and keep the pie in the oven for five more minutes. Remove the pie from the oven, and let it cool on a wire rack for at least 2 hours. Serve (or refrigerate to make more firm).

TURMERIC CHOCOLATE CHIP FRUIT MASH

Yield 1 serving

My daughter loves fruit mashes for their texture and fruity sweetness.

- *1 ripe banana, peeled and chopped*
- *1 teaspoon MCT oil (or melted coconut oil)*
- *1/4 to 1/2 teaspoon ground turmeric (or curcumin extract) powder*
- *1 orange, peeled, seeded, and chopped*
- *1/4 cup almonds, chopped*
- *1 tablespoon dark chocolate chips*

Mash the banana, MCT oil, and turmeric together with a fork. Fold in the remaining ingredients.

PART VIII
HEALTH

TURMERIC WHITENING TOOTH PASTE

Yield 1 use

Yes, this actually whitens your teeth in spite of turmeric staining everything else. It's good for their health, too, especially if you suffer from gingivitis or a toothache.

- *1/4 teaspoon coconut oil or grass-fed ghee*
- *1 pinch ground turmeric (or curcumin extract) powder*
- *1 pinch sea salt*

Bear in mind this will stain your toothbrush yellow/orange, but not your teeth. Why? Because it's magic.

Stir the ingredients together in a small dish and brush your teeth with the resulting mixture. If possible, let the mixture sit on your teeth for a few minutes. Spit the mixture out of your mouth and rinse. If there's any resulting yellow tinge after, it will go away with thorough rinsing. If you get yellow around the mouth or on hands, use soap and water to remove.

It might take repeated use to see results.

TURMERIC OLIVE OIL PULLING

Yield 1 use

Oil pulling is a process where you swish oil in your mouth for up to 20 minutes without swallowing it. It's reputed to have a multitude of benefits for your teeth, gums, and overall health. Adding turmeric to my oil pulling routine adds extra whitening power and more anti-inflammatory properties. I do this a couple of times a week, usually mid-day while I'm doing dishes and cleaning the house, but many people opt to do it first thing in the morning.

- *2 to 3 teaspoons extra virgin olive oil**
- *1/4 teaspoon ground turmeric (or curcumin extract) powder*

Mix the oil and turmeric together in a small cup or bowl. Transfer to a large spoon to pour into your mouth. Swish for up to 20 minutes, without swallowing it. When you're done, whether it's 5 minutes or 20 minutes, spit it out into the trash. You can rinse your mouth or brush with a toothbrush. Oil pulling daily or even weekly can have great benefits to your oral health and overall health.

* You can use grass-fed ghee, coconut oil, MCT oil, sesame oil, almond oil, or olive oil. I prefer olive oil because I always have it on hand and because it pours easily at room temperature.

TURMERIC GINGER TINCTURE

Consuming turmeric (and ginger in this case) in a tincture format can be great for fighting inflammation and increasing immunity and overall health. A few bonuses for tinctures is that they're convenient to take (just squirt it in your mouth or a cup of water), they travel easily, and tinctures can last for years.

You can buy turmeric (and/or ginger) tinctures online (I like Herb Pharm on Amazon.com). However, if you'd like to make your own, here are some guidelines.

Buy fresh, organic ginger root and fresh, organic turmeric root (about one half-pound of each). Grate them. Place the grated roots in a glass mason jar, filling the jar no more than half full with the grated turmeric and ginger. Fill to the top with 80 (or 100) proof alcohol. Place a lid on it. Place a label on it with the ingredients and the date. Set it on your counter for 6 to 8 weeks, out of direct sunlight, and shake it daily. (If you miss a few days of shaking it because you go out of town, that's okay.)

After the 6 to 8 weeks, strain off the liquid and store the resulting liquid extract in glass tincture bottles (you can buy them online or in most health food stores), or any bottle or jar, in a dark cool cupboard. Throw away the shredded roots.

A general rule for dosage to boost health is one dropperful, one to three times a day. As with many supplements and tinctures, it's a good idea to cycle off them for a week every three weeks. If you have more questions regarding dosages for specific ailments, consult a nutrition-minded doctor.

CONCLUSION & FREE PDF

With this book, you're now ready to take advantage of all the health benefits of turmeric. This powerful superfood spice, used regularly, will enhance your foods with powerful anti-inflammatory goodness. And you now have plenty of inspiring ways to use it! Enjoy your adventure into the world of turmeric.

I hope you've found this book to be helpful and that you add lots of turmeric to your life!

I'd like to send you a free gift, my ebook, *Easy Gluten-Free Cookbook*. Just email me at kristen@globalkristen.com and mention the title of this book (Turmeric Cookbook).

Did you enjoy this book?

If so, please leave a review at Amazon!

As an independent author, your reviews are extremely helpful in getting the word out. After you leave a review, please drop me a line at kristen@globalkristen.com so I can thank you!

∽

Kristen's blog at: GlobalKristen.com

Twitter: @KristensRaw

Instagram: global_kristen

Printed in Great Britain
by Amazon